To...

May you always stand in the light.

T0346478

The Light's Way

By Judy Pelikan

Abbeville Press   Publishers
New York ~ London ~ Paris

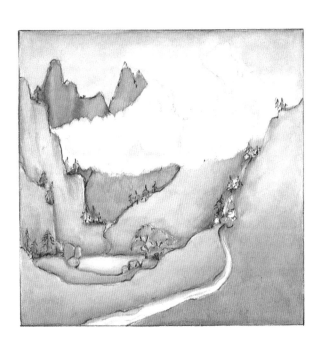

If you want to be warmed by the sun,
you must stand in the light.

First Edition

2   4   6   8   10   9   7   5   3   1

ISBN 0-7892-0138-0